Why Accountants Make *GREAT* ENTREPRENEURS

Bonus! - As a way of saying thanks, here's a short book that is guaranteed to excel your business career. It helped me greatly and will do the same for you if you can internalise the concepts.

Download Here → *http://goo.gl/iYx5aC*

Join Our Insider List

Get Our Premium Books Below for Only 99 Cents!

Join Here ^ http://goo.gl/wcNCvW

Insiders get Discounts to our Upcoming Book Titles upon Book Launch.

COMING SOON

9 ONLINE BUSINESS IDEAS THAT WILL STILL BE HUGE IN 2016

From a SIX Figure Internet Entrepreneur

Written By:

Mateen S

Brought to you by AffEngineer.com

www.AffEngineer.com Copyright © 2015 by AffEngineer Publishing

Disclaimer

No part of this publication may be reproduced or transmitted in any form or by any means, mechanical or electronic, including photocopying or recording, or by any information storage and retrieval system, or transmitted by email without permission in writing from the publisher.

While all attempts have been made to verify the information provided in this publication, neither the author nor the publisher assumes any responsibility for errors, omissions or contrary interpretations of the subject matter herein.

This book is for entertainment purposes only. The views expressed are those of the author alone, and should not be taken as expert instruction or commands. The reader is responsible for his or her own actions.

Adherence to all applicable laws and regulations, including international, federal, state and local laws governing professional licensing, business practices, advertising and all other aspects of doing business in the US, Canada or any other jurisdiction is the sole responsibility of the purchaser or reader.

Neither the author nor the publisher assumes any responsibility or liability whatsoever on the behalf of the purchaser or reader of these materials.

Any perceived slight of any individual or organization is purely unintentional.

Table of Contents

Why Accountants make GREAT Entrepreneurs

When I was employed full-time as a graduate engineer, I saw many people come and go with the company. I worked there for 2 years, straight of university before I bit the bullet and decided to plunge into entrepreneurship.

While working there, I'd notice a bunch of different personalties, how they worked and the trending strengths and weakness of each personality type. Of course there are many variables in peoples character that will ultimately determine the success/failure of a person but if certain people could just get their head together and get in the right mind set, they can definitely make it work.

Accountants are one of them.

I remember when my department manager was leaving his position and he was looking for someone to replace him. As it was an engineering firm, heavy in construction activities, I assumed they'd be looking for someone with a bug construction background. I was shocked to find out they were looking for someone who had a strong accounting background.

Now, 2-3 years into my Internet Marketing Journey and over 150k spent on advertising, I understand why. I understand why, no matter what the activities of your business are, the most important questions is, ***"Are You Making Money?"***, and to be able to put all the details away and look at <u>just</u> the numbers, is a skill set not many are trained to do.

They know the value of data

Almost anything in the world can be broken down and analysed through data. There's a saying,

"What doesn't get measured, doesn't improve"

This can't me more true in entrepreneurship. Whatever you do, if you can put it in numerical form and understand it stripping away all the detail then you'll be able to make better decisions on where your business is going.

My dominant activities in my business is a lot of FaceBook marketing. I spend most of my time reading reports and understanding how my marketing efforts are working. Whether the numerics look right or whether there are some improvements that can be made that will get me above average or great results.

I'm always looking at things like CTR, (Click Through Rates), Frequencies, (How often people have seen my ads), spends/revenue, cost per leads, cost per sale, etc. If you don't know how to understand this or don't respect this data you won't be able to scale your business in areas it can be scaled.
Accountants look at data on a daily basis. They can plot graphs and tables to drill down into weak areas or strong areas. They can see what parts of the

business needs attention, what parts of the business needs to go and can recognise connections between data that most people won't be able to understand.

They're used to Working Long Hours

Between the small amount of accountants I know, they ALL work long hours. It seems there are ample things to do in the accounting industry no matter what type of accountant you are.

I used to know people who'd work 10 hour days, go home and still be available via phone to do more work if need be! I personally don't know how they do it.

When I first started my business, I was working 10-12 hour days to make things work. I'd wake up at random times in the night to work on an idea I was excited about. Most of my work energy was motivated through desperation of wanting to make it work and excitement of the potential of my new ideas.

Now however, I work 4-6 hours, nothing close to what I used to but it's still enough to grow my business.

At the start, most people don't know what to do with all their spare time. As an accoutant, you don't hesitate to get straight to business. They can work all day on things to better understand their business. Working long is normal to them and although, just like anyone, they would prefer working shorter hours, they'll be fine working long hours at the start to get things working.

Many people that quit their day jobs to start entrepreneurship get so much spare time and end up doing a whole lot of nothing in it. Many people who quit their day jobs to try make entrepreneurship work do so because their bored/stuck at their current jobs. This boredom trains them how to waste time and so when they quit work and end up at home expecting to work on their business, they'll do what they've trained themselves to do. Waste time.

A good accountant who provided value to his company should know not to waste time. They should be able to get straight into it for hours. Lost in their own work and getting the necessary things done.

Like I mentioned before in time, you'll probably work less hours once you are comfortable with your time input vs revenue generation ratio. That is, 'how much time you need to work per day to sustain a revenue/net you're happy with.

It may vary everyday. Some days, I'll work 10 hours, simply because I have an idea that needs to be implemented or my work activities are directly contributing to immediate growth of my business and I need to work hard and fast to capitalise on this. Whatever the case an Accountant should be able to adapt to crunch time if need be.

They're Used to Staring at Computer Screens

Ok, maybe your sick of staring at a computer screen. I understand that, especially when you're working on someone else business. There's nothing like being stuck doing things for companies because you HAVE to.

It's a different story when you're doing it for your OWN business. Something you know is directly contributing to your own success and not someone else's who just pays you a salary.

Much of my entrepreneur life has been spent doing things on the computer. Coding, emailing, Designing, Marketing, almost everything happens on computers these days. I used to work in the Construction side of engineering so I'd be 60% in the office doing things on the computer and 40% on site.

I found it easy to continue working on a computer. In fact I preferred it to be that way. It's the lazy mans way of making money.

As an accountant who has spend much of his or her work life on a computer, it should be relatively easy to keep this habit when need be. Sure, get out and do your offline activities but when it comes to crunch time on the computer, accountants can deliver.

Know how to Cut Losses and Move On

I've seen many types of entrepreneurs in my Marketing Career. One type seems to be the most common. A type that doesn't go far and for good reason.

The type I'm referring to here is the emotional businessman. They're someone who can't deal with being wrong or are too in love with their product to let go, and that's the worst quality of business.

Business requires you to be cold some times. Not towards others, but towards yourself. Numbers don't lie and if you are unable to detach your emotions with your business model then chances are, you'll make decisions that are unhealthy for your business.

To expand and grow, you HAVE to be able to weed out what's not working and focus on what IS working. Whether you've spent hours or days or months on a certain project doesn't matter. If it doesn't work or give the results it needs to give for a certain period of time, you have to be brave and cold enough to cut it out of your business process.

I've seen almost every Shark Tank episode there is out there and notice a common reaction from the

Sharks when the above type comes in to pitch their business.

It usually turns out that this person has put in their life savings in this product, have spent years and years perfecting it but when it comes to the numbers there are almost NO sales to show.

The reaction from the Sharks is a reaction of shock and a little pity. Shocked because of obsessed this person is about their business idea that they're oblivious to the fact that it clearly doesn't work. A little pity because they know the sacrifices that have been made to get to this point and it definitely wasn't easy getting there.

As an accountant, I would hope you'd know better. An accountant should be able to understand everything in numbers form. If they're about to reach or exceed their test budget for a certain idea, they should be able to let go of it and start anew. Ideas fail much too often, in fact 95% of the ideas I've tried have failed. It's the 5% of ones that have made me a healthy six figures.

There is gain in those losses though, but their not in the form of money. Through the crashing down of ideas, comes a more focussed and learned mind. One that has cleared the space of some clutter and can focus in on something else. One that has the capacity to learn WHY their previous venture failed and not make the same mistake again. Repeat this process a dozen times and you will see success sooner than later.

When I first started I had a myriad of ideas. I had an idea list I was determined to get through. My first few months were spent trying 5-10 business ideas all at the same time. It wasn't long before I realised I was going no where with this approach. A large part of business is about focus, and if you're not able to do it, you will not develop the necessary habits and rituals to reach your goals.

For example, last year – 2015, I had only ONE goal. To hit 150k profit in the Internet Marketing Business. My mind was obsessed about this goal. I'd think of it when I was in the shower, during work, while out with friends. Slowly, I changed the food I ate so I can wake up earlier, be fresher, and think more clearly. I changed the time I slept, the people I hung out with, the type of short work goals I set, I changed almost EVERYTHING to suit this goal.

By the end of the year something wonderful happened. Someone who had barely made 5k in his previous year in his business ventures, hit AUD$150k+ in profit. Around $143k U.S. Which ever currency you take, the achievement was a big one. Most of the 12 months that year was spent in profit and it was the most hard working year I've ever had.

I remember, at the start of the year, when I still had no clue how to achieve this goal I would put my current ideas out there and see what people thought of them. Not to people that were close to me and would show love and pity and simply say yes so I wouldn't feel upset but to random people. To communities who couldn't care less about my feelings and would give me their honest opinion about the idea.

I'd go to reddit forums and post my idea in the relevant forum. If people loved it, they'd sa so, if they felt it needed some tweaks to be appealing, they'd say so, if they thought it was absolute crap, they'd say so. You NEED this criticism. You don't want to be deluded, you want to filter through all the clutter and get to the honest truth so you can make REAL decisions of the direction you want your business to go.

Nowadays, when I have an idea, I'll ask a few people who would be potential customers and ask them if they'd buy the service. I'd tell them to be brutally honest and tell me if it's crap. I'd much rather it this way so I don't spend my precious time on things that are going nowhere.

Moral of the story, be focussed, be cold to yourself, be a real entrepreneur.

Understand the Importance of the Process

When I worked in construction as a Junior Project Engineer, I'd do a bunch of tasks that to me, would seem unnecessary. I was young and had no idea how the corporate world work. Actually, I think it's more accurate to say that I thought I knew how the corporate world worked but in reality I had no idea.

I remember my first task was go through a certain department of the company and ask the 5-10 employees there how exactly do they do their work. What does their work and job role consist of and basically map out the whole process.

To me, a first year graduate engineer who was trained to manage construction and ensure this company was making money this task made no sense whatsoever.

It turned out the manager who had hired me was new and was planning on restructuring this certain department. The restructure would mean that certain people would be given different roles and some others would be fired.

My manager had no clue on how this certain department worked and so wanted to map everything out so new people can go through this process and quickly know what needs to be done and to whom they need to go to get certain tasks approved, etc.

Sure enough, new people did come in and my process maps were the first thing they were given. My process maps that I thought were a piece of useless information that would be stored away, were actually the core documents used to train new employees and get this department back on its feet.

It was after this experience I learned the importance of processes. The importance of sticking to a work model that was proven to work and slowly tweak certain elements to see if It improves the business model. This is the process of spit testing and we'll get into it later.

Process maps are mostly in the mind and after a certain while, you'll find your own way of doing things that works best for you. To be able to map this process on paper or on computer and see if you can work on certain parts of it to make it better should be something that you naturally think of as an accountant.

Understand the Importance of KPI's

Businesses are often analysed via their KPI's, (Key Performance Indicators). KPI's are usually something like.

- Reach an annual turn over of $xxx, xxx in 2016
- Have only 10 customer complaints I 2016

In the most basic terminology I can think of, they're short term or long term goals that are numerically measured at any given time of the business.

Analysing KPI's will give you an indications of whether you're on track to meet your goals or not.

There are too many 'entrepreneurs' or 'wantrepreneurs' as they're often referred to in the community who just work on their business day in day out without every analysing where it's going. By analysing I don't mean just thinking about it, I mean writing it down on piece of paper and measuring how much money you've made, how much money you SHOULD have made and making a road map of activities that need to be done to get back on track.

An accountant should be familiar with monitoring numerics and data and should be able to evaluate their business on excel to see if they're meeting their

KPI's. Although KPI's are what big business incorporate to keep their employees working the way they need to, it's also a good thing to apply to yourself and your own business.

At the end of the day we still have a employer – employee relationship except it's between ourselves. We are the employer and also the employee. The employer in us will map things out, think of things to do, list down activities. The employee in us will get right down to work and make these activities happen.

You need to be able to switch between the two modes when you need to.

Understand how Different Departments come Together to Provide Value

The accountant of the construction company I worked for would gather the financial details of the separate departments in the company and compile different types of financial reports so the higher ups can see it.

It was a tough job with a lot of number gathering and crunching but a cool thing about it was he could see how each department came together to provide value to the front end customers.

The concept of providing value is foreign to many people and for the first time entrepreneur it will take some time to come to terms with.

Every big successful entrepreneur out there, the Richard Bransons and Steve Jobs of the world will tell you to 'provide value to your customer and always be on the look out to make their experience better.

This didn't make sense to me for a long time. For far too long I was focussed on, 'how can this business make me more money', which is not 100% wrong but if you want to have a sustainable business that grows, you will need to grasp the concept of value.

After I started to see 'providing value' as something important, I noticed a big change in customer responses and realised why certain businesses work better than others.

Most of last year was spent selling custom apparel using FaceBook marketing. I generated $300k in revenue just doing this and used a variety of manufacturing companies for product fulfilment and customer support. It always turned out that one particular company, Teespring, would continue to be at the top and have raving fans.

Other companies would try and get in to the action but most of them wouldn't go far as eventually people realised the product quality was low, shipping times were low, too many times they'd get the wrong product and customer support was non existent.

It was all the opposite for Teespring. They're customers and affiliates were their first priority. They made sure they were ALWAYS happy. I remember I spent almost 2k promoting one of their merchandise which got taken down and my sales were reversed. After some back and forth emails they were happy to cover my marketing costs and take my loss.

Compare this with a company saying tough luck and having me take the loss. I continued to work with them and still generate money for their platform.

At the end of the day they provided better value to me as their customer/partner and this made all the difference. Multiply this one scenario to 1,000s of others and you'll have 1000s of raving fans and easily, a multi-million dollar company.

Moral of the story is to take a step back, put yourself in the shoes of your customer and see if you'd like the service you're providing. Be honest with yourself and make any improvements you can.

Know How Companies Work - The Big Picture

This point is related to the above. Being able to gather financial reports and other such reports from other departments, a corporate accountant has the ability to see how the inner workings of the company directly contribute to it making money.

Not many people in the world will be trusted with complete, transparent finances of companies. To be able to look at them and see where companies focus their spending and where the majority of their earnings come from is a blessing.

An accountant that works for himself, for example, would be able to compare different businesses and see trends in what makes certain businesses earn more then others. After a few years in the industry and after analysing 100s if not 1000s of businesses they'd be well suited to begin business for themselves.

In the internet marketing industry, many people keep their dominant resources secret so they don't become saturated with competition. The longer they keep their business activities on the down low, the longer they'll make money and the more of it they'll make.

Being able to see not only where the money is going and coming from in certain companies but how much is being spent with them gives great insight into the direct contributors to what makes the company successful.

For example, if a dog wash company is spending 10% of its marketing efforts on Google and 90% of it's marketing efforts on FaceBook, it's safe to assume that FaceBook is giving them good business.

If you see this trend with other dog wash companies then maybe FaceBook is a great platform to expand dog wash company operations! If you want to jump in the business, you'll know where to spend your money to get customers which is more than half the battle.

Even smaller things like how much is spent on overheads, how many employees are needed to manage a certain business, what's the average cost of an employee in certain roles, having all this information laid out to you is a huge advantage.

Have Access to What Most People Don't – Data/Numbers

This related to the above point. You have to remember that there is almost no other occupation that has access to the data you do.

As an accountant that will be able to see the breakdown of finances to certain companies, you're already at an advantage over others in business. Business is all about keeping ahead of the competition. Being able to invest time and money in new opportunities before anyone else does is a big part of being successful.

The average entrepreneur would have come from a corporate job, hammering away at the same task that provide no self development value, over and over again. These guys will jump in to business with no clue where to spend their time and money. They'll spend the next year or so trying to figure this out.

Of course, where business spend and receive their money is different for every business and the always changing business landscape means nothing will stay the same BUT most things will and this is key.

As an Internet Marketer, I have access to different

bits of knowledge. From the direct cost of business products to how they receive their customers. I need this knowledge in order to know how to make them grow their business and in order to fulfil my job efficiently I will need raw business information. I use this to my advantage by just being mindful of the average costs of products and marketing efforts that work for certain types of businesses.

Moral of the story, Never overlook how your strengths can be used to keep you ahead of the game or at the very least give you a boost when you first jump into business. A good start in business may mean the difference to long term success or failure.

Attention to Detail

This is probably the reason I could never be an accountant. When I'd give my financial report summary to my corporate accountant so he could compile it for his master spreadsheets he'd send to the higher ups, he'd always find issues in it that I would have somehow overlooked.

Whether they'd be small things like wrong job numbers or not including the dollar signs to big things like a completely wrong number input that would throw off the finance totals.

I could never be as attentive as my corporate accountant. Maybe I had way too many things on my mind as I was answering calls, running around and making sure everything was running smoothly on the construction site or maybe I was just not fit to be attentive while number crunching, whatever it was, my accountant was definitely better at it then anyone else in the office and that's a definite bonus in the business world.

Business requires you to keep a keen eye out for opportunities. These opportunities will present themselves in the form of ideas that randomly pop up into your head inspired by seeing something on the internet or TV or in the form of laying it all out on excel and spotting areas that can be improved or cut. The ability to calmly focus in on this is important and is something not everyone can do.

Even now, I'll miss things that will end up costing me. From forgetting to discontinue my advertising campaigns on Facebook, which sometimes has costed me 1000's to realising late that certain traffic sources were costing me more then they were making me.

I'd say I'm average at spreadsheet analysis but to be able to take it that one step further and lock in on things that would save me money would have gone a long way in making me a better entrepreneur. Something Accountants are already trained in.

Can Use IT Programs that are Beneficial

This one is pretty obvious and should have been placed somewhere at the start. It's no surprise that accountants can use a variety of number oriented softwares. Simple things like Microsoft Office, Visio and average understanding of the internet is a huge advantage over others.

A lot of business is done online and on the computer in general these days and to be able to use these tools at an adequate level are essential for the successful entrepreneur.

But that's not enough. Plotting complex charts that analyse every detail of business will have you spending too much time staring at data and little time doing the most important tasks like getting sales. As long as you know how to make simple formulae functions work for you on Microsoft Excel and plot graphs/charts if you need to, you're way ahead of many others.

When I worked in construction, (You'll be hearing that phrase a lot), a lot of my time was spent making plans on Microsoft project and analysing our cost/activity data on Microsoft Excel. Overtime, I got quite adept at it and it became easy for me to quickly plot something of value on these tools.

I still remember when on site supervisors needed to come in and get some office work done, they had no clue how to make simple tables or even send a basic email! I guess they had different strengths and weaknesses but the reality is, in this day and age, if you can't work around a computer to fulfil simple – semi complex work functions then you're at a severe disadvantage over others.

Accountants should be able to use these programs with ease, quickly plotting graphs and charts if they need to analyse a set of data. For my business, data is everything. Almost all my expenditures are marketing expenses necessary to learn about my demographic and how they respond. I get this information back in the form of numbers and can quickly make a helpful spreadsheet if need be.

Client Communication

As an accountant, chances are, you have a variety of clients that you need to service in order to keep business running. Even if there aren't many, even one client is enough to train you on customer service and what's necessary to keep them satisfied.

Sending an email has a different effect to making a phone call. These differences are learned on the job.

Even small things like referring to people by their name can make a big difference in the way your clients respond to you and how they perceive their business.

My current accountant takes her time to explain tax complexities to me, in a simple, yet informative manner. She may charge slightly more than other tax accountants but this value she provides me with allows me to better understand the business world.

I've recommended at least 10 people to her just because of how much I value her service and each reference has thanked me for the recommendation. She's obviously been in the game for a while and has leaned how to treat people.

Your clients are powerful marketing machines if you treat them right. They'll interact with many people throughout their life and if each one loves the way you treat them then you won't have to spend a penny on marketing because of the recommendations you're getting.

Hopefully, your accountant life would have taught you the above skills, if not, it will be drilled into you in your first couple of years in business.

Being Organised

This point relates to the 'being focused' point I bought up earlier.

While I was at university, I worked for an insurance company who were transitioning into using soft copies instead of hard. Meaning, they wanted to get rid of all the paperwork they'd get by issuing their clients policies and have them all online so they can be opened and access when ever they want. My job was to scan 1000's of these policies into the right folders while doing a bunch of other tasks.

It was an easy role but I had to be very attentive to detail or I'd scan policies in random folders where they'd get lost essentially meaning that particular client had no policy with us! It was a big screw up if it happened so overtime I learned to be more organised.

My manager then would often tell me that 'organisation is the key', and it stuck in my head since then. Small things like, keeping your desktop clean and documents in easy to read folders were now important to me. Previously I had documents everywhere and had never thought of how much time I was wasting while looking for them all.

As an accountant, you would have needed to be organised. From your computer desktop to your work desk you would have learned how to place things in places that are easily accessible and how to use posted notes and other such organisation paper tools to your disposal.

I've seen some peoples work desks, and they're a complete mess. Maybe some people can work like that but I can't. I need to know where things are, they make me more efficient and I'll achieve more that way.

A clean work space is a clean mind. When I work into a clean work desk, I'm ready to get straight into work. When I walk into a semi-messy work desk, I often spend some time on FaceBook and other time wasting activities. There's something about being organised that's healthy for the mind and keeps you doing tasks that are good and beneficial.

Time Management

Time management skills are drilled into you early as an accountant. In fact, it was drilled into me even earlier when I was studying for my degree at university and would often have to juggle exams, tests and assignments all days apart from one other.

Very quickly, you become overwhelmed with university work and one of the most important skill to get through it is to know how to manage your time so you can deliever each assessment successfully.

I would imagine these activities would become more serious in the accountant world where assignments and exams would translate to finishing financial reports in time.

As an entrepreneur, particularly working for yourself full-time, you can easily get lost in activities that provide no real value for your business endeavours. Being able to time-manage yourself correctly will stop you from working on these 'filler' tasks and applying the 80/20 rule to your business.

The 80/20 rule is working on the 20% of the tasks that bring you 80% of your revenue. It's a general rule but applies in most if not all business cases.

Most of the time, it's not a bunch of different clients or products that are contributing to your bottom dollar but just 1 or 2 big clients/products. Even in my case, out of the 100s of custom merchandise I designed and sold, it as just a couple that contributed to over 50% of my revenue.

Should I spend time working on selling more of these single products or should I have continued to find something else? Often it's best to stick to these big clients and products and to scale them as large as possible then it is to try find other things. Why would you not continue to scale what's already working?

Your road will split like this many times and this is where your time-management skills will come in play. After all, you only have so many hours in the day. You can't do everything. You'll need to figure out which tasks to prioritise and when to work on lower priority tasks and this where all those years of time-management training will come into effect.

Teamwork

Good teamwork is a delicate balance between getting things done and still maintaining a strong relationship with your partners or employees. Many times, accountants will request a bunch of information from their work colleagues which are necessary for them to fulfil their roles. Being able to do this without getting on peoples nerves while still communicating the importance of getting things done is a skill you learn while working with others.

As an entrepreneur, you may be a leader or you may be on the receiving end of business plans, either way you will need to cooperate and work in the best interest of the business.

We all want to be heard and it definitely is annoying when we feel there's a better way to do things sometimes things don't go our way and you'll need to do things a certain way to keep important parties happy.

This is where teamwork comes into play.

I've seem so many people who want to start a business and do it THEIR way. Most of the time you're wrong about your assumptions and if you're not open to this fact then you'll limit how much you grow and earn in your business.

A good entrepreneur is humble enough to ask for honest opinions amongst his/her colleagues or employees and to evaluate these opinions based on whether they make sense or not.

Teamwork should be ingrained into an accountant who would have only been able to successfully fulfil his work duties as long as this skill set is strong.

Things to be Weary of

There are definitely some things that make accountants great entrepreneurs but at the same time, there are some qualities that can be considered weaknesses to the entrepreneur with an accounting background.

This book would not be complete if I didn't state some of them as the goal of this book was to prepare you for entrepreneurship if you ever take the plunge.

Below, I'll list a few points that come to mind.

Used to tracking trends at successful companies, might not be able to cope with failure

Most accountants are perfectionists at heart. This mostly comes from the 'attention to detail' skill that's trained as an accountant. This is a good skill to have but if not managed properly might contribute heavily to giving up completely.

It took me a while to realise that failure was an important part of business. I wouldn't consider myself a perfectionist in fact I'm quite happy with something being imperfect but still out there making me money.

In many cases, you'll find that you don't have to fill every piece of detail or get everything right for your product or service to succeed. In fact, 70% of the small detailed tasks can be left out and worked on later.

This might not apply to all business but it certainly did to mine.

An example would be, when I was making custom merchandise for different niches. I'd make something for people that love Chihuahuas and I'd make another design for people that like fish.

Sometimes, I'd make designs for a completely different niche such as trucks.

For FaceBook Newsfeed advertising you HAVE to have a FaceBook page attached to the marketing advertisement and so the question arose whether I should have a separate page for each design or just one page with all designs?

Even though having a separate page would slightly improve my sales, it would be just way too time consuming to do this. It turned out to be a much better decision to just have one generic page with the sole purpose of selling shirts and focus on spending my time making new designs. The time I saved not making individual FaceBook Pages was better spent making more designs and although I may have been losing 1% in sales due to this 'imperfection' I was probably making an extra 5-10% due to me being able to launch more designs.

It's small things like these that might be a mental hurdle that's hard to overcome. Perfectionism occurs through the constant customer feedback of your product. Apple wasn't the Apple you see it today when it first started. Neither was almost every other successful product. Almost all successful products you see today are a result of constant re-iterations and fixes identified by customer feedback and putting the product out there to see how it performs.

No product is perfect from it's initial launch and this needs to be understood and internalised by every entrepreneur. It's a much better idea to get a product out there and try generate sales and THEN work on perfecting the product then it is to work on the product till it's 'perfect'.

Too Analytical

There's a common term in the entrepreneurship world used to describe people that lack action. It's something that happens to almost everyone at the start. It's called 'Paralysis by Analysis'.

This term refers to when there's too much reading, analysing and reverse engineering going on and too little real action. You will only get closer to acheving your goal by jumping in and doing what needs to be done. This could mean,

- Learning how to make a website, MAKING the website and promoting it
- Spending money to market your product/services
- Cold calling customers
- Writing out the ebook that's been on your mind for months

Whatever it is, get straight into it. Don't spend too much time trying to figure out how you're going to go about it, what niche you're going to tackle, what keywords you're going to include in your article/website name, what your logo is going to look like, these are all semi-important.

They're definitely not as important as just picking

something, jumping in, and learning from your mistakes.

An accountant, same as any qualified office profession that analyses data knows the importance of data but may have a difficult time turning this data into action. In fact, although data and numbers is good, these should simply be occasional reference points you look at every now and then. 80% of your activities should revolve around getting customers and getting the work done.

I know this was a hurdle for me hence why I've mentioned it. When I first started, I'd spend weeks just reading and days to decide on little things like the above. It took me some time that, although I was learning, I'd forget most of it in time and get no where closer to my goal. It's not good enough to know how Richard Branson made his riches or what healthy business habits Donald Trump has to build a multi-billion dollar business.

At one point I had banned myself from reading blogs and listening to podcasts because of how much time I was spending on them.

You're ONLY going to get closer to your goal by putting these learnings into practice. At the start it's going to be tough because there's so much to learn but eventually you'll be able to do things much quicker then most people.

The beauty about this business is that skills are directly transferable and so if you ditch your first business venture, you can transfer your learnings onto your next giving it a better fighting chance then the first.

Most people quit after their first 'failure'. This is the worst thing you can do! You're SUPPOSED to fail at the start. It's how it works. Just like how you'd get 90% of the questions wrong when you start studying for an exam. As the exams get closer and you learn how to get most of your questions right, you'll be at a much better position on exam day. Come exam day, and a pass will be easy for you.

This is how entrepreneurship works. You try, you fail, you learn, repeat. Do this at 100% focus for 3 years and you would have reached your goals 3 x over.

Getting out & Hands on, (Getting Sales)

The business world consists of a variety of tasks. Things from building websites to cold calling potential customers. Most people will begin with what's more comfortable for them.

If you've worked as a website developer, chances are, the first thing that will spring to your mind when thinking to start your business is to make a website. It's only fitting you do what you can do best first.

If you're a designer, chances are, you'll want to design logos and banners, prints and things that you will apply to your business.

If you're an accountant or engineer however, much of your initial activities will most likely be a lot of planning, forecasting figures and goal setting. Although this is good and our profession has trained us to be great at these activities, they should only form a small percentage of your work activities.

The hardest part about business is getting sales. So after the necessary planning and research get straight into getting customer sales or feedback. Even if your product isn't ready, try get something working as soon as possible and put it out there for people to judge whether they think it's valuable or not. Some examples of how this works.

Before writing a 100 page eBook that will take you around 2 weeks to complete, make a cover for it and spend some money on advertising to see if you can get people to opt-in for a discount when the book is released. This could be simple FaceBook advertising to a sales page with the cover of the book on it.

If you're spending $10 per opt-in, maybe your book idea isn't a good one. If you're spending only $1 per opt-in then hey, you might be on to something.

This is called 'validating your idea' and it's done BEFORE you start working on a project. Once your idea is validated then get a product out and start selling. Over time you'll understand that sales and customer value is all that matters. Instead of making a fancy website, spend that money on making a website that's simple, clean, straight to the point and has the best sales/opt-in conversion rate you can possibly get. Just because something looks nice doesn't mean it's good for business.

If your business is an offline one, cold call 100-200 potential customers and pitch them your product. See if anyone is interested or better yet, if you can get any sales. A lot of people shy away from cold calling and it's understandable as to why but cold calling is still one of the most effective ways to find potential clients. Not many companies do it, and those that do, don't know how to do it right.

When I was looking for a job as a Civil Engineering Graduate, I had applied online to at least 80-100 companies. I received rejection letters from most and for those that I was able to get an interview for, there was just way too much competition and with no work experience at all it seemed impossible.

I decided to do something no one was probably doing at the time and that was to pick up the phone, find my local directory and call EVERY company that employs Civil Engineering grads. In 2 days, I called 400 companies, received at least 50 requests for my resume and found a placement at a construction firm that built mansions in the most prestige suburb in Melbourne. 2 Weeks later, one of the largest construction company in Melbourne called me in for an interview, eventually ending up doing my 2 year graduate program with them.

You see, I had to get out of my comfort zone to get ahead of my competition and it payed of big time. It seemed the more I was willing to do what others weren't the more I'd find gold nuggets that haven't been mined yet. I was terrified at the start of picking up the phone and calling that first company but 10 calls later it was easy. Business is all about conquering your fears and almost everyday you'll be tested with a variety of tasks that will force you out of your comfort zone.

In the business world this translates to doing tasks that will have the biggest effect on your business. I know people who's first business expenditure was $500 on a logo design before they started any business related activities. Seriously, $500? You can spend that money on FaceBook marketing to try obtain customers or to see if your business idea has any merit.

Might not be able to take it if they get things Wrong

I don't think anyone who gets into business truly understands how many road blocks their going to encounter. They may have heard that failure is part of the process but what does this actually mean? I'll try illustrate the meaning with my personal experience.

When I was designing merchandise, my initial success:fail ratio was about 1:15. Meaning, out of 16 designs ONLY 1 will make me a profit. The other 15 won't get me any customers or if it did, it would at a loss.

Eventually, as the landscape got harder, that ratio went to about 1:30 and right at the end of my work with this business I designed 200 prints and NONE sold. Can you imagine that? 200 times I made something thinking it would make me money but it didn't. I spend around $20 marketing each one to test whether they'd sell which translates to $4,000. That's fine, because if you compare these losses to the profits gained by working designs, they're small.

Many people that started the same business as mine, would make 3-4 designs and be disheartened that they were making a loss, eventually discontinuing the business. It took me 50 designs to get my first profitable one. Looking at people that quit after 3-4 designs, I can't help but shake my head at how little they're prepared for the business world.

The business world is all about the above. You'll go through a string of road blocks and hurdles that will make you want to quit on daily basis.

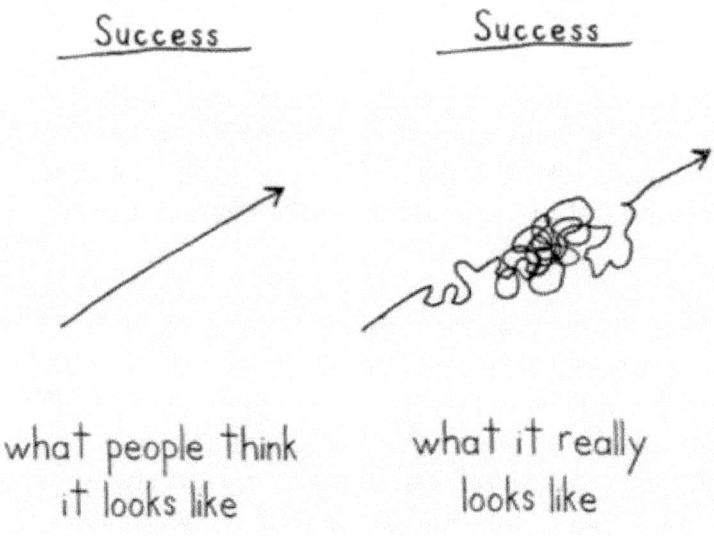

Success   Success

what people think   what it really
it looks like   looks like

Although there's not much happening on the outside, there's a lot of self-development happening on the inside. Your mind, whether you realise it or not, is taking note of things that work, things that don't, is getting trained to handle failure, to deal with risk and financial insecurities. To deal with the roller coaster ride we call entrepreneurship.

Accountants should be prepared for all this. They may have analysed data that's from a business that's working and is on it's feet not knowing how long it took for the business to get there. The profits/losses from a business that's already made it past the make or break stage of it's life cycle is very different to one that's starting out.

You have to remember that these businesses already have a working process that they've refined over years and after 100s of thousands spent on learning. Don't be disheartened if your business is not profiting right away. It's not meant to. Whether you like it or not, your business will also have to go through the make or break stage. This may last weeks or months, depending on your business model and your commitment to it.

Whatever the case just remember that the business world is riddled with failure. The idea is to fail quickly, and with minimal investment so you can learn, recover and grow from your mistakes.

Entrepreneur Tips If You Decide to make the Switch

Now, if your serious about this, there's somethings that I've realised through my few years of full-time business that will give you a boost at the start of your business career.

I'll list them below. Try and take a moment to think about each one and if you ever do decide to make the switch, they'll serve as good reference points or experiments to try.

Eating Healthy

People have mixed opinions about this and that's totally fine. I'll just tell you my own experience in the matter and the effect food has on my business routines.

You see, business is all about conquering yourself. What you practice in the real world will be your attitude in your business world.

I have an uncle who owns a multi-million dollar company. What he does at the age of 55 is very different to what my father or any of his other 4 brothers do. He gets up early, eats healthy, exercises and makes it a point to say hello and smile to everyone he walks past on his weekend mountain hikes.

I once went hiking with him up a huge mountain in Malaysia and although I was totally puffed out, my uncles was still running up the mountain like a trained hobbit from Lord of the Rings! I was totally amazed. He'd be the first person to lock eyes with a passer by, smile and try start a short conversation if we happened to rest together. It all started to make sense to me.

His business revolves around networking, building

relationships, negotiating and the like. What he does outside business makes it easier for him to perform his duties inside business.

The same applies to eating healthy. For a long time I ate whatever came my way, never thinking anything of it. It was just the way I lived and my body type would allow me to keep any weight from being put on. I was a relatively skinny kid and most of the time, my food intake didn't show at all.

These eating habits, followed me all throughout university and most of the day I'd feel lethargic and sleepy. I'd take naps at lectures, during breaks, as soon as I'd get home. I thought it was normal to feel like this, never really giving attention to food.

Then I quit work and had to be mentally focussed and ready so I didn't waste my day. During this time a friend of mine wanted to start a 'raw-diet' challenge where the only things we ate were raw fruits, veggies and nuts. Experimental me at the time thought it would be fun and so I joined him.

3 weeks in, I was on a totally different level. I thought more clearly, my energy levels were through the roof, I don't think I had ever felt any better.

I'd jump out of bed at 5.30am ready to work, take NO naps during the day, and be 100% focussed on whatever task was at hand. My ability to box longer while in the ring at training reached an all time high by a long shot and I was just flawed at how different the feeling of a healthy, ready mind felt. It was like I was living dead my whole life.

This experience made me incorporate healthy eating as priority number 1 in my business. I'll spend an hour making smoothies, cutting fruits and veggies, making juices and basically being prepared every day. If I eat junk, I'll have very little of it.

I highly recommend you to incorporate healthy eating into your routine. Almost every successful entrepreneur I know incorporates a somewhat healthy eating schedule. Anthony Robins starts his day with a green smoothie and has lemon water regularly.

Whatever it is, find something that works for you that you enjoy doing, do it for 2 weeks straight and see the benefits it gives you. Start small and gradually add something to the routine till your 100% happy with your diet. You'll see massive improvements in your life in general.

Waking Up Early

I was a totally different person in university. Sometimes I wonder how I even passed it. From eating garbage on a daily basis to sleeping late, I was doing everything wrong in the book.

Maybe there are some people that do well at the later hours of the day but not me. There's a certain point in the night that switches me into 'waste-time' mode and I can't do any work as a result of it.

Not to mention never feeling like your done with work. I like the feeling of getting work done and out of the way right in the morning so I can focus on other things like hanging out with friends or boxing training.

There used to be a time, when my diet was at it's best and I was waking up ready to work at 4am. I'd have a good 3 hours to myself with not a single sole disturbing me. Three hours of solid work is a LOT of work. If you were to compare how much actual work someone does in the office, you'd probably conclude, 'not much'. If you were to think of how much solid work is done, you'd get a number around 3-4 hours IF that. I know some days I'd go to work and be lucky to do 2 hours of solid work.

Waking up early allows you to get work done and out of the way. Imagine waking up at 5 and finishing work by 10am. By the time people have finished their morning coffees and are settling into work mode, you're done with work and are doing things that you actualy enjoy. You've earned the right to relax a bit, catch up with a friend, or take the rest of the day basically doing whatever you like. Not to mention you don't have to worry about work for the rest of the day!

This is the my approach to my work and it works wonders. The key to waking up early is to have a healthy diet and sleeping early. If you're not doing any of these two then you MIGHT be able to get out of bed in the morning but doing work is another story.

If you're a night person, I'd recommend trying the morning routine. Remember, you don't HAVE to work the whole day. If you can limit your work to be finished at a certain time around midday, you'll find yourself working hard to complete your work.

Learning Good Marketing

My first set of business ventures were mostly digital. From phone applications to building websites, I had a lot of great ideas and I had the work ethic to get them done but I started to realise that they all flopped because of poor, or in most cases ZERO marketing.

I thought you'd be able to just put your website or phone application up there, announce it on FaceBook and it would catch on like wildfire eventually having the whole western world finding it. I couldn't be further from the truth. I started to realise that making the product is the easy part, getting interested eyeballs who are willing to spend money on your product is where it gets tricky.

After 6 months of doing random phone apps and websites I decided to give it all up and focus 100% on Internet Marketing, commonly referred to as 'affiliate marketing'. Affiliate marketing is the process of bringing business to online companies and getting paid a commission, often as a %, for the sales you were directly responsible for. Think of it as a performance based salesman, only, on the online world.

This business model forced me to learn marketing

techniques that would bring in interested traffic who would actually buy the product. It was extremely difficult at first but now, 2 years in, it's a lot easier and gives my own business ideas a much better fighting chance. I now understand the importance of building an email list or customer base. Small things like knowing how to get traffic from FaceBook and marketing to test my products and ideas go a long way in saving me time with wasted ideas.

Marketing is essential for any business and is a direct contributor to the success and failure of a business. Whatever business you're in, I would recommend either learning digital marketing yourself, (there are ample tutorials on Youtube or you can visit my site for in-depth video tutorials on my website), or hiring a reputable marketing consultant to get you started right.

Whatever the case, don't underestimate the importance of marketing. You can have the best, most valuable product in the world but if you can prove this to people, it's useless.

Product Validation

This is a concept I briefly touched upon above. I've been guilty of working on projects for weeks or even months before even validating my idea! Now, looking back this seems so silly to me, especially knowing how valuable your time is.

My year designing shirts, I made almost 2,000 designs. From small variations to completely different designs, each could be validated and tested immediately to determine whether they were a good idea or not.

I would make 5-10 designs a day and drive $20-$30 worth of traffic to them via FaceBook seeing if anyone bought. If yes, I'd keep it, if no I'd ditch it. The next day, I'd throw another 5-10 designs under test mode and repeat the process. This forced me into the validation mentality. Product validation happened on a daily basis and in relatively large scale!

The beauty about the business model I was working with allowed me to do this while not worrying about printing the product, manufacturing, shipping, customer service etc.

Compare this with someone who has to do the

above all by themselves. The same time they'd test 5 products, I would have test 50. The more I tested, the more frequently I came across gold nuggets which I could quickly capitalise on. This made all the difference and taught me great marketing while making me a lot of money.

Noah Kagan is someone I follow regularly and as a successful entrepreneur he has a tonne of videos on Youtube that are extremely valuable to anyone new to the business world. He's HUGE on business validation and will validate his idea on the same day he comes up with it!

Validating is the process of testing whether your idea has any life in it or not. This is usually in the form of driving unbiased traffic to your product or service and seeing their response. Responses are generally in the form of how much it costs to get people to opt-in, to get a sale, whether people are commenting, sharing, etc.

Whatever you decide to do, validate it first. Let the real world decide whether or not your product is needed or not. You, as the creator of the product will obviously have an emotional attachment to it often blinding you of the realities of whether or not it's a good _business_ idea. Let the market decide this. Sometimes, it's brutal feedback, but this is what you need to grow and to get to the point you want to get. After all, it's the people that are buying your product not you.

Resources for business.

Block Yourself from Social Media

When you work for yourself you have to learn how to separate yourself from work and play. You can't do both together no matter who you are.

When you work, close all distractions. Turn your phone on silent, close FaceBook, snapchat, instagram or whatever social media website you regularly check and dedicate the next hour or so to work on ONE task. Set a timer. Timers create urgency and have always been an essential tool when I need to get work done.

Sometimes I don't check social media at all until I finish my work. This forces me to get my work done.

Most people don't realise how long it takes the mind to get back into work mode after it's been distracted. A small 2 minute social media session can knock another 5 minutes out of your work time. Imagine if you have 5-10 social media sessions in a 2 hour work period, how much time are you wasting?

Even things like emails can be looked at later. Emails and messages are really just peoples request for your time. Your time is valuable so spend it wisely. It's something you'll never ever get back and to just give it away to anyone that wants it is silly. We're busy people with important things to achieve.

No social media till work is done or only after a productive work session.

Being Productive

Productivity is one of the biggest hurdles to overcome when working for yourself. People think, when they quit work and being working for themselves they can work whenever they want and start involving themselves in all the fun activities they dreamt about at work.

Technically you can work whenever you want but without a strict routine, you'll find it very difficult to get work done.

When you have an option to do some work or do something fun, most people are going to do something fun. Not to say work isn't fun, but after awhile you'll want a break and how you manage your work-break timings is what determines how productive you are.

The reason why most people are productive at work when they need to be is because they have an *immediate* reward/punishment outcome from their activities. If you do your work, you'll earn your daily income, if you don't you'll most likely get fired if you keep it up for a few days.

With entrepreneurship it's completely different. There is very little immediate rewards. Sure, there are small wins but they mostly come in the form of fulfilling or reaching a short goal. What about money? When does that come about? In most cases you'll have to stick to a project or business idea for a while before it starts to bring you an income.

To be able to continue with it with the same enthusiasm everyday until you're making money from it is challenging and is a popular reason why most people give up.

You HAVE to have your own productivity rules when working for yourself. Rules like the below,

- Can ONLY work between 8-4. This simulates work and stops the 'I'll do it later', syndrome.
- Work with no distractions
- Do 2 hours of solid work before midday
- If you don't fulfil the above, you're not allowed to use your phone for a day
- Have a set number of things to achieve before your work is completed

I've used all these rules at some point of my career and many of them have been permanently incorporated into my routine. They work great but you HAVE to follow through. If you break the rules, you punish yourself, if you do your work, you reward yourself. Remember you are both an employee and an employee.

Persistence

This one is talked about by almost EVERY successful entrepreneur. It's a generic tip but I think no one really understand the scale of persistence needed to succeed with entrepreneurship.

Want to make money from building a website? Don't stop until you've tried at least 20 times.

Want to start internet marketing with FaceBook? Don't stop until you've launched at least 100 marketing campaigns and have spent 3k on advertising.

People usually fail because they don't continue with their idea. In many cases, the idea is solid but will take time to actualise. We've all heard the saying 'Rome wasn't built in a day' but many don't know how to apply it.

A successful business goes through 100s of road blocks and hurdles until it becomes successful. You have to be prepared to continue, as long as the idea is validated.

The initial months are the 'learning stages' of the business. Here is where you'll learn what needs to be fine tuned, what your customers actually want, how much it costs to acquire a customer, whether you can reduce this cost, etc. You're not _meant_ to be making a profit.

Give yourself this space, and you'll find entrepreneurship less stressful. The more you understand this concept, the more patient and persistent you'll be with your endeavours and the closer you'll get to reaching your goals.

Conclusion

Everyone will go through mostly the same phases when starting entrepreneurship. Whether you're an accountant or a tradesman, there are battles and hurdles to overcome for any personality type.

However, as outlined above, there are a lot of skills Accountants possess that make give them a huge competitive advantage over others. With the world turning more and more online, it's important to know how to work technology to improve your business processes.

If you're an accountant, which I'm sure many of you are, then I recommend you to start your journey towards entrepreneurship. The risks are great but if you stick to it long enough you WILL get there. With your set of skills, you should be able to adapt to the entrepreneurship life.

The reward of working for yourself is too sweet to be not tasted in this life. All it takes is a determined and focussed mind. Whatever you decide to do, I wish you the best!

- Mateen